What Are You Doing?

Shannon Lelli

What Are You Doing?
© 2021 by Shannon Lelli

You have one moment, one chance at this life.
You were created for a reason and a purpose.
There is so much more!

It's out there—as powerful as the wind, as awe-inspiring as the lightning and thunder, as infinite as the night sky, and as deep and wide as the ocean.

This is my story of how I found that "so much more."

Chapter 1:
It Only Takes a Moment

January 1, 2008 was a bitter, freezing day in the middle of nowhere, Pennsylvania. I woke up miserable and angry at my life, the world, and my husband. Feeling hopeless and stressed, I wondered how I had ever arrived at this place in my life. Maybe you have never been in a place like where I was that day, but for me and my family, it was terrifying.

We didn't have enough money to pay the mortgage that month, and we had over $60,000 worth of credit card debt wrapped around our necks. My husband, Anthony, was self-employed in construction. The housing market had crashed, and after waiting months to be paid by a large builder he'd worked for, the builder claimed bankruptcy, leaving our family in a financial mess. We'd just had our third baby in four years, so we had medical bills on top of credit-card debt (made even worse by a couple of ER visits with lousy insurance: a kidney stone for me and RSV for our baby).

On top of all this, my income was way down. I owned a smoothie shop that did well in the summer but provided no income during the winter. So we had no income, no money saved, bills piling up, and three little ones to feed, which left Anthony

and me in a financial hole much deeper than we had ever known. Additionally, I was seventy pounds overweight.

Stressed, angry, and miserable, I decided to throw myself into exercise. We had a Gazelle, the Tony Little infomercial machine, in our very small bedroom. I'd been using it as a clothing rack, but dug it out from under the clothes, and soon I was flinging my legs through the air and feeling better. At least I was doing *something*.

Ten minutes into my routine, I was starting to work up a sweat when this wonderful machine broke. Yup, the little piston holding it all together stopped holding it all together. And that's when I too fell apart. In a rage, I began cursing and then grabbed for my coat. I screamed to my husband I was going out for a run despite it being ten degrees outside.

As I ran, I also started screaming at God in my head. *How could this happen? How can I be in this place? How did we get into such a mess? And how will we ever get out of it?* I believed in God, or at least I thought I did. I would have even called myself a Christian. But at that point I was beginning to question everything.

At the time, I would have described my relationship with God as similar to a girl from Kansas who had never been to the ocean. She had seen pictures of the ocean, read books about it, and heard a lot of people talk about it, so she figured she knew all about it. But anyone who has actually gone into the ocean, felt the tug of the current beneath their feet, allowed the raw power of the waves to smash against their chest, and enjoyed the beauty of the vast shoreline could tell her she didn't know the ocean at all. That was where I was. I didn't know that I didn't know God at all.

As I continued running, I used music from my iPod to try to drown out my pain. I turned down a long road with farms on both sides, and soon wide-open dead fields spread out on both sides of me. Suddenly, both my knees seized up. I came to a screeching halt, completely immobilized.

Standing by the side of the road, about to freak out, I heard a voice as clear as day say to me, "Take off your iPod." I thought, *What in the world was that?* But I took out my ear buds. Then I heard a rushing sound, like a train coming up behind me, followed by the words, "Lean back."

So I did. And in leaning back, I realized the wind was holding me up, wrapping its arms around me. The Voice then whispered, "How much greater are you than the birds of the air? I feed them every day. Stop worrying and trust Me."

I knew God was speaking to me. I felt so overwhelmed with love as He just held me with the wind and spoke to me.

After what felt like an eternity, He said, "Go. Run." My knees unlocked and I could move again.

I ran all the way home, sobbing, and rushed up the stairs to find Anthony, who had just gotten out of the shower. "You're never going to believe what just happened!" I cried.

This was the day that, instead of just knowing *about* God, I really came to know Him. To experience Him.

Suddenly, I had a hunger to know all about this God who showed up in my pit of helplessness to tell me how much I was loved—and was not forgotten. And that everything was going to be okay if I would just trust Him.

I took my Bible out of the box where it was collecting dust on the shelf, and went looking for the words God had spoken to me. I found them in Matthew, as part of a promise from God for all of us.

> *"Therefore, I tell you, do not worry about your life, what you will eat or drink; or about your body, what you will wear. Is not life more than food, and the body more important than clothes? Look at the birds of the air; they do not sow or reap or store away in barns, and yet your heavenly Father feeds them. Are you not much more valuable than they? Who of you by worrying can add a single hour to his life?"* (Matthew 6:25–27)

Life is so valuable, and our time here on Earth so short, that I want everyone to experience the unfathomable ocean of God's love. He promises us that if we have faith as small as a mustard seed, we will see God do miracles in our life (see Matthew 17:20). We just have to trust Him. How exciting, scary, and freeing life becomes, all at once, when we do. When you're truly walking with God, you no longer worry about what happens next or care what everyone else is doing—because He's with you, and that's all that matters.

Don't rest until you stand in awe of the majesty of God around you, humbled by how small you are and how big He is. As He carries you into the unknown, that is where your life truly begins.

All of us are on a journey, trying to make sense of this life. Are you working for the weekend—or for a paycheck or a vacation? Have you ever considered that today could be your last day? What if you lived your entire life chasing after something—wealth, fame, a bigger house, a nicer car—only to find out those things don't matter? I can tell you right now that every material thing you are hoping for in this world isn't worth striving after.

No doubt you've already obtained some things in life that you thought would fulfill you. Perhaps you're already dreaming of more. If you're young, you can't wait to be older. If you're older, you wish you were young. If you're in school, you can't wait to graduate and get a job. When you have a job, you can't wait to retire. If you're single, you want to be married. When you're married, you might long to be single. If you don't have children, you can't wait to have some. When you have babies, you can't wait until they are older. When they're older, you wish they were young again. No matter your age, you wish you had done some things differently. When you're dying, you wonder what's next.

What *is* next? That's an important question to answer, because what's next should determine how we live today. As James, the brother of Jesus, wrote, *"Why, you do not even know what will happen tomorrow. What is your life? You are a mist that appears for a little while and then vanishes"* (James 4:14).

It's denial and complacency that keeps us from thinking about death even though it's a guaranteed coming event in our life. But since there are so many beliefs, religions, and spiritual ideas that try to explain what happens after we die, how can we ever be sure what's true—and know with certainty what is next?

I'm sharing my story because I now know without a doubt that God is real. His promises in the Bible about what comes next are all true. I don't know this because someone at church told me so. I know this because I met God on the lowest day of my life and He spoke to me. He has transformed me and my family. He has done more miracles in my life since then, more than I could ever recount in this small book.

God is real. He is so good, and He wants each of us to fall at His feet and allow Him to change *everything*. My story is just a glimpse into how God works in people's lives. Each of us is unique, and He works uniquely in each of us when we let Him. He promises that if we seek Him with all our heart, we will find Him (Jeremiah 29:13).

As you read further, I encourage you to put your religious upbringing and ideas about who God is on hold. Allow the living God the opportunity to speak to your heart and show you who He is and how much He loves you.

Chapter 2:
When the Power Begins

My life, and God's power in my life, began that day on the side of the road when I was twenty-nine years old.

On the outside, I had looked like I had it all together: a home, a husband, three wonderful kids, a loving extended family, and even my own business. But on the inside, I was a mess. I was on an emotional roller-coaster, happy one minute and then screaming at my kids the next. I put down my husband to make myself feel better. I tried a new diet just about every week. I was never truly happy, always looking for something to fill my cup.

That day on the side of the road, I saw how small I was. I also felt a love I had never experienced. I wanted to know this God who had spoken to me, and I chased after Him with all my heart. When I opened my Bible, I prayed, "God, please help me understand this book. Please give me wisdom. I want to know You."

The Bible came alive to me. I started to understand things that had once seemed to be written in another language. I learned so much about God, and it began to transform every area of my life. I started a daily journal, writing down all that He was teaching and showing me, and all the amazing miracles He does every day of my life. He even began to help me navigate through my family's financial mess. His advice was to just trust Him one day at a time.

So I trusted Him with everything I bought and every bill I paid. In the grocery store He showed me how to make inexpensive meals. I know that sounds crazy, but I would stand there and pray, *Lord, I have no idea what to buy with the little money I have.* He would show me that a bag of ramen noodles, a bag of frozen broccoli, and a rotisserie chicken chopped up would make an amazing soup. Also, peanut butter and jelly sandwiches for dinner never hurt anyone!

Once, I was standing at the checkout counter in a dollar store and God drew my attention to the checkout lady. As I paid my bill, He whispered to me, "Give her twenty dollars." I said in my mind, *That's crazy.* I heard, "Give her twenty dollars *and* the change. It is not your money; it's mine." So I gave her the money, and with a terrified, "God bless," I left the store.

I was learning—one day at a time—that if I wanted Him to help me, I had to give Him everything. Nothing was mine.

Even my weight battle was placed in His hands. From as far back as when I was six years old and in dance class, I was conscious of my weight. I wasn't little like all the other girls, and that self-consciousness of my size had followed me the rest of my life. God showed me that I needed to use the beautiful muscles He gave me and eat more of what He made (and less man-made food). One meal at a time, my inside transformation began to manifest on the outside. With His guidance I was able to get in the best shape I'd ever been in. Satan tempted Eve out of the gate with food, and he will tempt us too if we let him.

God even showed me how to better manage my business by putting myself on the schedule more. That way I saw firsthand how I could run a better, more efficient operation. I learned that the more control over my life I gave God, the more excitement, peace, and joy I received. And I've learned that I can't earn His love. What pleases Him the most is when I just sit at His feet and trust Him with my life, one moment at a time.

Slowly my heart began to change. If I yelled at my kids, I would get this unsettled feeling that told me, *That's not okay.* Soon God began sending strangers into my life for me to love. And then sending others to love me.

A life with God, I decided, is a lot like swimming in the ocean. It's big and scary and exciting at the same time, because you have no idea what will happen next. Like with the ocean, you just have to jump in. But not everyone does. Have you ever seen how crowded it is on the beach? Some people never go in the water. Some venture to the edge but then stop, while others go out just a bit more. And then there is always that one brave, adventurous person who swims way out past everyone. I would always see that person and think, *Wow, they're brave. It must be amazing out there, but that is too scary for me.*

The follower of Jesus is like that one person swimming fearlessly out beyond the waves. It's scary, because you're out where you've never gone before, all alone and without visible support, but it's so worth it. Still, to get up the courage to do that, you first need to look at where you are now. When I look around, I see four types of people who remind me of those on the beach. I call them the Spectator, the Wader, the Treader, and the Swimmer.

Which one are you? Let's see.

The **Spectator** is the person sitting on the beach blanket enjoying drinks and appetizers with the rest of humanity, sunning himself and having a good time. Are you him, having no interest in going near the water? Are you content and happy with life as you see it? Do you not want to even think about what happens after you die? Do you love celebrities and the ways of this world?

The **Wader** is the person at the water's edge, going in only far enough to get her feet wet. The minute the first wave threatens to engulf her, she jumps back to the safety of the beach. Are you like her? Do you wonder if there's a God out there somewhere? Do you feel like something is still missing in your life, but you're not sure it's worth the risk of finding out—because the security of the shoreline trumps getting in over your head?

The **Treader** is the one who is actually swimming. He has gone out farther than most. Spiritually, this person thinks, *I go to church, I read the Bible, and I know all about God and John 3:16 and what comes next. I'm all set. I asked Jesus into my heart.* The problem with being the Treader is he hasn't gone far enough; he's stopped right where the crashing waves (and Satan) can suck him under.

Who do you think Satan tries to attack? Not the Spectator or the Wader. He'd let them enjoy life on or near the shore. The Treader would be his target because the Treader actually wants to follow God. So Satan's strategy is to deceive the Treader into thinking he's doing all God wants, that he's gone as far as he needs to in order to please God.

And how does Satan get the Treader to believe this? With Scripture taken out of context. He makes the Treaders think that Jesus understands and accepts their half-hearted attempts to serve Him.

It's false teachers feeding us feel-good, unscriptural messages, which are more like self-help seminars, that keep us living like the rest of the world.

This is the *worst* place to be. This is the lie that keeps Christians from experiencing the power of God. Do you find yourself struggling with the same sins over and over? Do you believe you should be making disciples but don't know how? Do you sense God continually pushing you to look more like Christ, but feel stuck in the muck? That's where I was. And this is why we have so many people who ultimately give up and walk away from God. Because, unknown to them, they've been practicing fake "Christianity."

What we don't realize is that in treading water, we are right where Satan wants us. Because if we ever really launched out into the deep to truly follow God's path for our life, we'd then experience the true power of Jesus's resurrection and set the captives free.

Sadly, this is where most Christians are today—hanging back, trying to follow God in their own strength. And, as I discovered, God will let us stay there until we start to sink and cry out for help—really cry out. Because until we truly surrender, He usually won't come to rescue us.

So, the Treader may know that John 3:16 says, *"For God so loved the world that he gave his one and only Son,"* but it is far better to know what Jesus said in Revelation 3:15–16: *"I know your deeds, that you are neither cold nor hot. I wish you were either one or the other. So, because you are lukewarm—*

neither hot nor cold—I am about to spit you out of my mouth."

In reality, the Treader is in a worse place than the Spectator and the Wader. Because in thinking he is serving God, he is still stuck with all his unresolved struggles. His only hope is to try and fix them himself. And he becomes so focused on this that he doesn't think to let God—his only hope—fix him. This is hell on Earth. I know, because that's where I was before I met God by the side of the road.

As well, God says it is better to honestly reject Him than be lukewarm in our commitment. Again, that's where I was. I wasn't on fire for God. I had a little bit of God, but I was completely lukewarm, and I didn't even realize it. Satan had me all tied up in knots.

When the day of judgment comes, the Spectator and the Wader shouldn't be surprised. They knew all along that they were making a conscious choice to not move forward—and they will have to live with their decision. But you who truly want God's best but are only going part way should not forget that, *"It is written, 'As surely as I live, says the Lord, every knee will bow before me; every tongue will confess to God.' So then, each of us will give an account of ourselves to God'"* (Romans 14:11–12).

If we are *not* walking with God in full intimacy when the time comes, that moment will be awful. The Treader will no doubt be the one who will cry out, "Lord, Lord, I did so much for you!"

But what did Jesus say?

> *"Not everyone who says to me, 'Lord, Lord,' will enter the kingdom of heaven, **but only he who does the will of my Father who is in heaven**. Many will say to me on that day, 'Lord, Lord, did we not prophesy in your name, and in your name drive out demons and perform many miracles?' Then I will tell them plainly, 'I never knew you. Away from me you evildoers!'"* (Matthew 7:21–23)

Jesus didn't stop there. He went on to say,

> *"Therefore, everyone who hears these words of mine and puts them into practice is like a wise man who built his house on the rock. The rain came down, the streams rose, and the winds blew and beat against that house; yet it did not fall, because it had its foundation on the rock. But everyone who hears these words of mine and does not put them into practice is like a foolish man who built his house on sand. The rain came down, the streams rose, and*

*the winds blew and beat against that house,
and it fell with a great crash."* (Matthew
7:24–27)

The truth is, treading water is so much harder than floating or swimming. Treading water is exhausting; so is trying to *earn* your way into God's kingdom. Like treading, you never go anywhere. Satan is like the undertow of the waves. He will try and keep you from ever getting free to swim out into the ocean. No matter how much you give, serve, and try to change the world in your own strength, it won't accomplish the work of God. As Jesus said, *"The work of God is this: to believe in the one he has sent"* (John 6:29).

Our own efforts will never earn us a place in God's kingdom. We can't earn a free gift; otherwise, it is no longer a gift. *"For it is by grace you have been saved, through faith—and **this is not from yourselves**, it is the **gift of God**"* (Ephesians 2:8).

> *Therefore **no one** will be declared righteous in God's sight by the works of [religious] law; rather, through the law we become conscious of our sin....This righteousness is given through **faith in Jesus Christ** to **all** who believe. There is no difference between the Jew and those from the nations, for **all** have*

sinned and fall short of the glory of God.
(Romans 3:20–23)

The **Swimmer** is the one who is willing to go all out. To swim out beyond where her natural ability can take her. This is where reliance on the power of God begins.

I realized I could never be a Swimmer in my own strength. I was too weak. How tempting it was to stay close to shore where I thought I could control things. But then I realized I couldn't, so I decided to trust God and let Him take me to places I couldn't even imagine.

When I first started swimming, the waves were scary. The temptation to give up and turn back was strong. Satan whispered that if I kept going, I'd be pulled under. But I learned to call out to God to give me great strength to forge ahead. I learned His many promises were bigger than the waves and the whispers of the Enemy. These promises became my water wings. There was nothing that could stop me from overcoming. And in the process, I learned to know Him and love Him, trusting Him more each day.

He has since taken me farther and farther out from the safety of the shore—that is, my reliance on the things of this world. The temptations grew smaller and weaker, and God's faithfulness grew larger and stronger. His power and strength in my life is holding me up. It is like floating on the water with the glorious sun shining on my face. No matter what storm comes, I'm learning how to lean back and float over them in His arms. I've learned that "*The LORD is my light and my salvation—whom shall I fear? The LORD is the stronghold of my life—of whom shall I be afraid?*" (Psalm 27:1).

When you experience God in this way, you can't help but tell everyone how amazing He is. Life becomes an incredible journey when you know He has you in the palm of his hand. You want everyone to experience the freedom, power, and love that only He can give. You have confidence that no matter what storm comes along, God will *never* let you go.

> *Therefore, my brothers and sisters, make every effort to confirm your calling and election. For if you do these things, you will never stumble, and you will receive a rich welcome into the eternal kingdom of our Lord and Savior Jesus Christ.* (2 Peter 1:10–11)

Who are you—the Spectator, the Wader, the Treader, or the Swimmer?

Chapter 3:
Ready for the Storm

After that day on the side of the road, my life was turned upside down—or, more correctly, right side up. I started reading my Bible every day. I had always had trouble understanding the Bible, so I prayed, *God, please help me to understand. I want to know You. Please show me who You are.* And He did. As my understanding grew, my heart began to change. I no longer wanted what I wanted; now I wanted what God wanted.

Galatians 2:20 says this best: *"I have been crucified with Christ and I no longer live, but Christ lives in me."* I was learning to die to myself and my old ways, and learning to fully trust God with everything. This was no small commitment. It's a transformation that I know will continue, causing me to look and act more and more like Jesus, until the day I die. In the meantime, it's preparing me to weather the storms of life. (Which was good, because even though I didn't know it, a Category 5 hurricane was headed my way.)

Throughout this early transformation in my life, my husband stood beside me. He saw change, he saw miracles, and he joined in Bible studies we would have at our house and worship in our backyard. He believed God was real, but down deep he thought he was a good person already. Until the day the walls came crumbling down.

The truth is my marriage to Anthony was blah. We didn't fight a lot, but we weren't very intimate either. We were both so busy with our lives that the condition of our marriage was left to simmer on the back burner. I worked, took care of our (now) four kids, and ran the home. He worked, worked, and worked some more. I knew we were drifting apart, and our conversations increasingly had a negative undertone. I avoided talking to him because he always seemed so grumpy, and finally, prompted by God, I suggested we get marriage counseling. I encouraged him to choose the counselor, and eventually he did.

At first, counseling helped. We started communicating and dating again. I looked forward to our sessions and felt God's hand on the whole thing. I learned all the areas where I was failing our marriage. All seemed happy in our home again, and then—*kaboom*! The hurricane hit.

I discovered my husband had been having an affair for a year. He had even been texting this other woman right under my nose—even while we were sitting on the couch after our counseling session. My world came crashing down, and I felt crushed into a million pieces. I never would have expected this in a million years. A year. A whole year of lies. A whole year of betrayal. How could I have been so blind?

I ran straight to God. I threw myself on my bedroom floor, crying out to Him full of anger, sorrow, hopelessness, and pain like I'd never known. But oh how quickly God met me. In that moment I knew He was holding me, comforting me in His arms. In that moment He became my strength. He surrounded me in the most beautiful, unbelievable way. As painful as that experience was, I'd return to that moment a hundred times over if I could experience His presence that way again. I really would.

But I wasn't out of the woods yet. I said, "Lord, I want to lock all the doors and throw his clothes out the second story window. I hate him. I don't even know who he is!"

God whispered in my ear, "Trust Me. Trust Me one moment at a time. I have something so amazing for your family."

This was a promise I had to lean on with all my heart—even when nothing made sense. But I knew how faithful God had been to me up to that point. He had always done everything He had promised, and He was asking me to trust him again. He was now the only one I could trust—the only one I knew who would not betray me.

When I confronted Anthony about the affair, he was very remorseful. He said that when the counseling started going well and our relationship was improving, he didn't know how to get out of the affair. He asked if I could forgive him.

I praised God that we were already in counseling, seeing God's hand even in that. It wasn't easy to just forget his betrayal. There were days where I didn't see how we could ever heal. I would cry out to God, "I can't do this!" And He would give me strength that I didn't even know was possible.

He would tell me to text Anthony "I love you." And I would tell him no. And God would whisper back, "Trust me." Just getting my kids' breakfast or sitting at the table for dinner would have been impossible in my own strength. But God was constantly at my side, giving me a peace and a joy I cannot explain. He is so good! So amazing! I want everyone to experience His "peace ... which transcends all understanding" (Philippians 4:7).

My driving force became caring only about what God thought of me. Obeying and following His lead was all that mattered. If this marriage could be put back together, only He could do it. And He did. I was finally able to completely forgive Anthony, and our marriage is better today than it ever was. He showed me how to take it one day at a time.

The months that followed were a whirlwind. God kept me very busy, but I noticed Anthony's life became increasingly difficult. God was purifying him in ways only He can do (Anthony will have to write his side of the story one day).

About nine months after the hurricane hit my life, we were trying to plan a family vacation right before school started. Anthony suggested, "Let's rent a camper for a week." To me, that idea sounded terrible. I hated camping. But God was teaching me that I needed to trust Him to lead my husband—and trust Anthony to lead our family (even though he was not a believer yet). So we rented a camper and drove to upstate New York. It was *amazing*! We had no cell phone service, no electronics—just pure family time in the middle of nowhere.

God somehow used that camping trip to do a major restoration in my marriage. I don't know how it happened, but He did it! My family was restored to be even closer than before. How was this possible? How could I not hold resentment and unforgiveness and distrust or a slew of negative thoughts toward my husband? How could we all be together in a small space and have the most amazing time together as a family? Only God... only His power could transform the darkness of a situation like mine to light.

When we returned from that trip, I had a burning desire to take our family on a camping trip across the United States. The only problem was that Anthony was reluctant. Besides, we didn't have a camper. And I had a business with no one to run it in my absence. Plus, we'd have to pull the kids out of school for two months.

But I knew my God was bigger and more powerful than any obstacle. If it was His will for our family to take a cross-country trip, then it would happen.

The kids and I started praying about it. They would pray, "God, please soften daddy's heart to do whatever You want us to do. Please provide a camper. And please provide a worker for our smoothie shop who loves our store and can be there anytime."

A month went by, and one day God put in my mind a camper that I didn't think existed: it would be under $15,000, have low mileage, sleep six, have a back bedroom with a door, and be able to get us across the country and back without breaking down. When I looked at campers, they were all in the $20,000+ range. I would then remind the Lord that He had said under $15,000, right? (I must drive Him crazy sometimes. Ha-ha.)

Soon after, I got an email from a young woman who had just graduated from college. She said she loved my store and was available to work anytime. I interviewed her and hired her on the spot, and she said she'd be ready to start that Saturday, in two days.

The next day, Anthony came home from work miserable, just hating his job. That night I looked at RV Trader and what did I see? A camper for $14,999 that slept six, had a back bedroom with a door, and had only 15,000 miles of use. And the next thing I heard was my reluctant husband saying, "Let's go see it."

So, that Saturday morning we drove two and a half hours out to Lancaster County, Pennsylvania, to see this camper. One look made my heart melt and gave me goosebumps from head to toe. As Anthony took the camper for a test drive around the block, with the kids and I riding in the back, I was praising God, saying, "God, you are so amazing. This is crazy. Why are you so good to me?"

When we arrived back at the lot, Anthony looked at me and said, "Let's do it. Let's take the kids across the country." Thank you, Lord!

We all went out to lunch to celebrate. After a while I looked at my watch, and when I saw what time it was, I panicked. I had to be at the store to train the new girl at five—and we were two and a half hours away. We jumped in the car and drove straight to my store.

She was already there, waiting for me. I introduced my family to Natalie, and my kids and husband watched me train her to run the store—which was a first. One day. Every single prayer was answered in one day.

Two months later, my family piled into our new camper to go across the country. God took us on an adventure of a lifetime and showed all of us how to trust Him, to let go of all the things of this world and just trust Him.

> *Now all glory to God, who is able, through his mighty power at work within us to accomplish **infinitely more than we might ask or think**.* (Ephesians 3:20 NLT)

Chapter 4:
New Every Morning

On my spiritual journey, one of the most valuable lessons I've learned is how Satan wants to destroy us. Satan has infected our entire world system down to the food we put into our bodies. He is not a little red dude with a pitchfork. He operates in a very different way. Jesus calls him "the deceiver" and "the father of lies." The definition of *deceive* is to cause someone to believe something is true that is not true, typically to gain some personal advantage.

What is Satan's personal advantage? We are either working for his kingdom or for God's. God talks about Satan in the Bible, and says, "*You were blameless in your ways from the day you were created till wickedness was found in you*" (Ezekiel 28:15). The Bible tells us that Satan "*said in his heart*" that he would make himself above God (Isaiah 14:13).

Satan was with God, but because of his sin he was cast down from the mountain of God. He took a third of the angels with him. This was the start of the spiritual battle that we now find ourselves in. It is the battle of good and evil that continues in everything— every movie, every book, every thought in each of our minds. No one gets out of this battle. Satan wants to win souls and won't stop until he deceives all whom he can.

The biggest questions I had when I started to read the Bible and know God was, why aren't more Christians telling everyone about how amazing God is? And why do most Christians look and act like everyone else in the world when we're supposed to have the power of God living inside of us? Why aren't Christians the light of the world?

One word: Satan. So many Christians are walking around under Satan's control and don't even know it. If I ask a Christian about their faith, they will usually tell me what church they go to.

What in the world is "church"? The Bible says it is the body of believers that worships God in both truth and spirit. We come together to build each other up so we can go out to be the light of the world and make disciples. After God opened my eyes and I looked at the way we do church, I thought, *This doesn't make any sense.* People gather together in the typical church each Sunday, they say good morning, sit like spectators at a show for one hour (like on the beach), and go home to watch football. For so many, Christianity is something you do one hour a week in a building—not something you do seven days a week out in the world.

The last thing Satan wants is for God's people to gather together and rely on the Holy Spirit to worship Him, and for teaching and direction for service. If we did these things, we might actually experience the power of God and wake up. We might actually see God show up and begin to transform us, and then send us out to transform our entire community—or nation. And wreak havoc on satan's kingdom while building God's!

The greatest deception of our day, I believe, is that for us to gather together, we need a talented, seminary-trained professional; a building; a big band, lots of money; special effects; and even a coffee bar. Who needs God to show up when you have all that?

When we don't rely on God, our kids will soon see right through our fake religious gatherings. And when they grow up, they are easy pickings for Satan to get them to throw God out with the religious bathwater. They'll say, "It's just as fake as the Easter Bunny and Santa." And Satan wins again. His thoughts are more dangerous than his pitchfork.

But we can't say we weren't warned. Jesus told us:

> *"The thief comes only to steal, and to kill, and to destroy. I came that they may have life and have it abundantly. I am the good shepherd. The good shepherd lays down his life for the sheep. He who is a hired hand and not a shepherd, who does not own the sheep, sees*

the wolf coming and leaves the sheep and
flees, and the wolf snatches them and scatters
them. He flees because he is a hired hand and
cares nothing for the sheep. I am the good
shepherd. I know my own and my own know
me, just as the Father knows me and I know
the Father; and I lay down my life for the
sheep." (John 10:10–15 ESV)

The choice we must make every day is, *Will I*
let myself be deceived by the lies of the devil who only
wants to steal, kill, and destroy? Or will I cling to the
good shepherd because He is the only one who truly
loves me? The one who makes me lie down in green
pastures and gives me life in abundance.

Spend some time with God, His Word, and a
journal beside you. I can guarantee that you will be
flooded with all the other things you should be
doing. The more truth you get in your heart, and the
more you know about God and our Savior Jesus
Christ, the quicker you will spot Satan's lies and
schemes. And the more power you will have to
overcome.

We have gone so far off course from where
God intended his church to be. But God knew this
would happen, and inspired the apostle Paul to
prophesy this warning:

But understand this, that in the last days there will come times of difficulty. For people will be lovers of self, lovers of money, proud, arrogant, abusive, disobedient to their parents, ungrateful, unholy, heartless, unappeasable, slanderous, without self-control, brutal, not loving good, treacherous, reckless, swollen with conceit, lovers of pleasure rather than lovers of God, **having the appearance of godliness, but denying its power. Avoid such people.** (2 Timothy 3:1–17 ESV).

That last line is the most terrifying: "*having the appearance of godliness but denying its power.*" If that doesn't describe most churches, I don't know what does. Where else do you find people who claim to be godly but there is no evidence of God in their lives? Where else do people honor Him with their lips, but their heart is far from Him?

Is God's power evident in you? Do you see His power reigning over every aspect of your life— your work, your home, your marriage, your children, your finances, your struggles?

Paul prayed:

I keep asking that the God of our Lord Jesus Christ, the glorious Father, may give you the Spirit of wisdom and revelation, so that you may know Him better. I pray also that the eyes of your heart may be enlightened in order that you may know the hope to which He has called you, the riches of his glorious inheritance in the saints, and his **incomparably** *great power for us who believe.* (Ephesians 1:17–19)

Incomparable means there is nothing to compare it to. We have no idea what God has in store for us when we start to believe. Become a dedicated disciple of Jesus and His incomparable power will be evident in you—and the world will begin to see less of you and more of Jesus.

Therefore, we do not lose heart, but though the outer man is decaying, yet our inner man is being renewed day by day. For momentary light affliction is producing for us an eternal weight of glory far beyond all comparison, while we look not at the things that are seen, but at the things that are not seen; for the things that are seen are temporal, but the things which are not seen are eternal. (2 Corinthians. 4:16–18 NASB)

There are no promises the Christian life will be an easy road, however. Suffering comes with the package; it's the way God cleanses us of sin and self, so we are going to have days when God tests our resolve. Some days we will succeed, and some days we will be back in the flesh and act ugly. Some days we will spot Satan's lies and tell him to flee, and some days we will succumb to his temptations.

When we fail God and sin, we need to know what to do next. Satan will be quick to condemn us, which makes us feel like we'll never get it right. This keeps us from going to God and repenting and receiving forgiveness, knowing *"there is now no condemnation for those who are in Christ Jesus"* (Romans 8:1). We can't forget that *"the steadfast love of the LORD never ceases; that His mercies never come to an end; they are new every morning; great is your faithfulness"* (Lamentations 3:22–23 ESV).

One of my favorite chapters in the Bible is Luke 15. There, Jesus tells three parables about things that are lost, starting with a sheep and a coin, and how after each one is found, there is great rejoicing. The chapter concludes with a man's lost son who takes the entire inheritance his father gives him, leaves home, and ends up in a pigsty. But the son finally repents and returns to his father. Despite all the son did, the father forgives him and rejoices and throws a huge party for him.

This is how God feels about us. He says, *"If my people, who are called by my name, will humble themselves and pray and seek my face and turn from their wicked ways, then I will hear from heaven, and I will forgive their sin and I will heal their land*" (2 Chronicles 7:14).

Chapter 5:
Success

I see now that God's idea of success is so different from the world's, which is measured mostly in terms of how much money and goods a person can acquire in life. As the popular expression goes: "The person who has the most toys, wins!"

To those who consider themselves successful according to the world's standard, Jesus has this to say: "*You say, 'I am rich, I have acquired wealth and do not need a thing,' But you do not realize that you are wretched, pitiful, poor, blind and naked*" (Revelation 3:17). He then instructs them with these words: "*I counsel you to buy from me gold refined in the fire, so you can become rich, and white clothes to wear, so you can cover your shameful nakedness, and salve to put on your eyes, so you can see*" (v. 18).

Jesus wants to give us so much more than what the world has to offer. But we will not experience true success until we first realize how empty and meaningless the world's rewards are—and repent and turn away from our pursuit of them. That, too, is a gift of God.

"Those whom I love I rebuke and discipline. So be earnest and repent. Here I am! I stand at the door and knock. If anyone hears my voice and opens the door, I will come in and eat with that person, and they with me. To the one who is victorious, I will give the right to sit with me on my throne, just as I was victorious and sat down with my Father on his throne. Whoever has ears, let them hear what the Spirit says to the churches." (Revelation 3:19–22)

Success with God begins when we finally give Him total control of everything in our life. And everything means *everything*. Every decision, every care and concern, every dollar in your bank account, everything we own or will own, along with our jobs, children, and spouse. Even our life itself. Those things will no longer be our ultimate responsibility. They will be His, and He will manage it all so much better than we ever would or could.

Every day is a gift. We should start each one by thanking God we even woke up. Who do we think we are, if the first thing we utter when we awake—and take the first breath God allowed us to breathe today—is, "I want..." Jesus is our example of what it means to lay down our life. Paul tells us to live the same way: *"Finally, dear brothers and sisters, we urge you in the name of the Lord Jesus to live in a way that pleases God, as we have taught you"* (1 Thessalonians 4:1 NLT).

God has called us to live holy lives as Jesus did— not impure, self-centered lives. Anyone who lives according to God's standard of righteousness—and not according to some human teaching—will be saved from the coming judgment: *"For God has not destined us for wrath, but to obtain salvation through our Lord Jesus Christ"* (1Thessalonians 5:9 ESV).

I've heard Christians excuse their sinful behavior by saying, "Well, we aren't Jesus. We can't live as perfectly as he did." True. But we do have the same Holy Spirit that lived in Him to lead us, teach us, correct us, and encourage us to keep going. We may not do it perfectly at first, but we should be getting better every day. That is how we become sanctified, by allowing the Holy Spirit to disciple us so that our light shines brighter and brighter.

Romans 12:2 says that we are to grow into the fullness of Christ: *"Don't copy the behavior and customs of this world, but let God transform you into a new person by changing the way you think. Then you will learn to know God's will for you, which is good and pleasing and perfect"* (NLT). Changing the *way* we think is critical. It is through the mind that Satan ensnares us and keeps us from obeying God. He plants lies in our head based on fear, or worldly wisdom like "I'm too old, I'm not gifted, I'm not capable, I'll look foolish, there's an easier way, etc." Any of these lies, if we believe them, will knock us off track.

Satan will also try to get us to measure our "goodness" by comparing ourselves to everyone other than Christ, who should be our only standard of righteousness. Satan will cause us to judge others by their faults so we think we're not so bad. Or he'll condemn us for not doing as much as that brother or sister who is doing more than we are. Either way, we're deceived and kept from becoming the person God wants us to be. All because we listened to Satan. Thank God for our advocate in heaven, Jesus Christ!

> *My dear children, I am writing this to you so that you will not sin [disobey God]. But if anyone does sin, we have an advocate who pleads our case before the Father. He is Jesus Christ, the one who is truly righteous. He himself is the sacrifice that atones for our sins—and not only our sins but the sins of all the world."* (1 John 2:1–2 NLT)

The evidence that we've been deceived is when we say, "I know God," but we don't obey His commandments. That makes us a liar. We're not living in the truth. Only those who continue to obey God's Word truly show how completely they know and love Him. And when we stumble, we have the remedy: *"If we confess our sins, he is faithful and just to forgive us our sins and cleanse us from all unrighteousness"* (1 John 1:9).

I'm not a Bible scholar, but I know that God has changed every aspect of my life through continual reading of the Bible along with the conviction of the Holy Spirit. I am no longer the same person I was. My heart wants to do only the will of my Father in heaven, and nothing can separate me from His love. This isn't a joke; this is so serious. No one is promised tomorrow, and how we choose to live today effects our eternity.

Living for Christ isn't a bumper-sticker saying or something we add to our life. It's a new life entirely. Jesus can change our approach to everything—the words we speak, the movies we watch, the music we listen to, and the things we do with our time. It's all about doing the will of our Father who sent His Son Jesus to become the answer to a broken world. He has the power to transform our lives if we let Him. It's our job to go and make disciples of the nations (Matthew 28:19). But how can we make disciples unless we're first discipled ourselves?

Being a follower of Christ is not easy. The Bible makes this clear: *"You can enter God's Kingdom only through the narrow gate. The highway to hell is broad, and its gate is wide for the many who choose that way. But the gateway to life is very narrow and the road is difficult, and only a few ever find it*" (Matthew 7:13–14 NLT). Jesus tells us there will surely be suffering: "*Everyone will hate you because you are my followers. But the one who endures to the end will be saved*" (Mark 13:13 NLT). That's how we become overcomers. And through it all, God will watch over and protect us.

> *How great is the goodness you have stored up for those who fear you. You lavish it on those who come to you for protection, blessing them before the watching world. You hide them in the shelter of your presence, from those who conspire against them.* (Psalm 31:19 NLT)

If Christians would pick up their cross and follow Jesus the way He wants us to, it would impact this world in an amazing way. We are all like lame beggars. Without Jesus, we can't walk uprightly. But Jesus came to heal us and get us on our feet so we can "*run and not grow weary*" (Isaiah 40:31 NIV), sharing the good news about Him. Praying for the sick, casting out demons, and telling people about God's coming kingdom. That is the reason God put us here. That is our job that will ultimately determine our success or failure.

We don't realize how quickly we can be deceived into making the things around us our god.

Whatever motivates us to get out of bed in the morning is our god. It can be our kids, job, money, fitness, or success. Even working in ministry can become our god or idol. But nothing should come before God Himself—*nothing*. Not even the Bible. That's why we need the power of the Holy Spirit operating in our life to convict us and give us direction each day. *"You will receive power when the Holy Spirit comes on you; and you will be my witnesses in Jerusalem, and in all Judea and Samaria, and to the ends of the earth"* (Acts 1:8).

Is this power in your life now? Do you want this power and guarantee of salvation? It is a gift from God for those who believe: *"For the promise is for you and your children and for all who are far off, everyone whom the Lord our God calls to himself"* (Acts 2:39 ESV). And it is the presence of the Holy Spirit that marks us as His: *"When you believed, you were marked in him with a seal, the promised Holy Spirit, who is a deposit guaranteeing our inheritance"* (Ephesians 1:13–14).

Have you been marked in Him?

Chapter 6:
A Challenge

You've made it this far, so I want to challenge you. I know that God is beyond amazing, and I know how He answers prayers in unbelievable ways. That's why I'm challenging everyone who is a Spectator, a Wader, or a Treader to become a Swimmer. And I'm encouraging everyone who is a Swimmer to keep swimming and ask God to encourage all those around you out into the deep.

This new life I have been speaking of is a life of faith, and it begins with a step of faith. So why not start today? Get on your knees before the God of the universe and let Him hear your heart's cry to know Him. Saying, forgive me God for thinking I was god and I don't want to do this life on my own. Allow Him to change everything in the best way possible.

"But whenever someone turns to the Lord, the veil is taken away." (2 Corinthians 3:16) When the power of God takes over your life you will see you were blind before and you didn't even know it. The transforming power of God removes the *"veil"* or a cover from our eyes and takes us from death to life. At the end of our life (which could be today for any one of us), it won't matter how much money we've earned, what car we drove, or what accomplishments we've made. All that will matter is

did we live for our will or for God's, who promised us an eternal future: *"'Not everyone who calls out to me, 'Lord! Lord!' will enter the Kingdom of Heaven. Only those who actually do the will of my Father in heaven will enter."* (Matthew 7:21).

I pray that God will open your eyes to see Him more clearly every day. May you see how amazing He is—so much so that you will want to share who He is with everyone around you. As you begin to walk with God and trust Him like a child it works a lot like when a child is learning to walk. You will fall down, but cry out to God and He will pick you up. As you walk you get stronger, you fall less and less and then you start helping others to walk. This is one day, one step at a time but God promises to be with you through it all.

*"Now may the God of peace-
who brought up from the dead our Lord Jesus,
the great Shepherd of the sheep,
and ratified an eternal covenant with his blood -
may he equip you with all you
need for doing his will.
May he produce in you, through the power of Jesus Christ, every good thing that is pleasing*

to him. All glory to him forever and ever.
Amen.
(Hebrews 13:20–21)

So I ask you...

What are you doing that will last for eternity?